Mirror Eyes

An Eclectic Book of Poems

Susan Tuttle

Susan Tuttle

Copyright © 1957-2017 Susan Tuttle

All rights reserved. No parts of this publication may be reproduced, stored in a retrieval system, or transmitted in any form or by any means, electronic, mechanical, photocopying, recording, or otherwise, without the prior written permission of the copyright owner, except for short quotations for review purposes.

This book is sold subject to the condition that it shall not, by way of trade or otherwise, be lent, resold, hired out, or otherwise circulated without the publisher's prior consent in any form of binding or cover other than that in which it is published and without a similar condition including this condition being imposed on the subsequent purchaser. Under no circumstances may any part of this book be photocopied for resale.

Cover design by Aaron Kondziela: www.aaronkondziela.com

A WriterWithin Publication

www.writerwithinpubs.com

ISBN-10: 1-941465-21-8

ISBN-13: 978-1-941465-21-9

Dedication

This volume is dedicated to the wonderful poets who have so enriched my life: Shirley Radcliff Bruton, Debra Davis Hinkle, Brandy McKay, Janice Konstantinidis, Evelyn Cole, Anne Peterson, and Bonnie Young.

Susan Tuttle

Mirror Eyes

Contents

Introduction 1

Section One: An Eclectic Mix
- Paradise 6
- Night Music 7
- Breaking Point 9
- Centennial Dreams 10
- For My Son, Aaron 12
- Whine 14
- The Miracle 15
- Together 15
- Vertigo 16
- The Garden Cat 17
- Book Covers 19
- Dinner Time 21
- Dreamscape 23
- Luna Life 24
- Envy 25
- Everlasting 27
- Becoming in Los Osos, Ca 29
- Labyrinth Light 34
- Love Story 36
- Mirror Eyes 37
- Mourning 39

One Fond Farewell.................................... 40
One Spring... 41
Soft Skin.. 42
Storm Surge.. 45
Summer Place.. 47
Premonition... 48
Musing on the Muse.............................. 49
Boredom... 50
Perambulations...................................... 52

Section Two: For Ted
Consequences.. 55
Corridor of Time....................................55
Aftermath...56
The Night of Blood................................ 58
For Ted... 59
Summer of '72..60

Section Three: Song Lyrics
The Dream of Love................................ 64
All You Can Give Me.............................65
Be Still... 67
He Knows..69
Take My Hand, O Lord......................... 72
Come to the Table of Love................... 74
Love One Another..................................76
Come Worship Our God (Day)............. 78
Come Worship Our God (Night).......... 79
I Am The Way.. 80

You Are a Lamp..82
Where Will He Be Born Tonight?...............83
Christmas Is For Children........................... 86
I've Gone Home.. 88

About the Author.. 91
Fiction Publications...................................... 94
Nonfiction Publications............................... 95
Poetry.. 95
Spiritual Publications.................................. 96

Mirror Eyes

INTRODUCTION

I grew up in Buffalo, New York and knew I wanted to be a writer when I was in fifth grade. I had written a 2-verse poem in class—when I was supposed to be working on math homework!—that I was pretty pleased with. (To be honest, I thought it was the best poem ever written, but then, I was only ten years old.) I showed it to the school crossing guard, who said it was really good. She asked for a copy, and I gave her one.

Without telling me, she sent it in to our local paper, the now-defunct Courier Express, where it was printed in the Olaf Fub Sez column. I'd had no idea she had submitted it. What a surprise and thrill to see my poem, and my name, in the paper where everyone could see it.

A week later, the paper forwarded a "fan" letter from a reader who lived about 45 miles away. He told me "Paradise" meant so much to him that he had cut it out and pinned it up on his wall, so he could read it every day.

That did it for me. If I could move people, if I could make a difference, just by putting words on paper, that was what I wanted to do with my life.

In the beginning poetry poured out of me, as well as some short stories and vignettes. I filled two school notebooks with poems. I had a poem published in almost every issue of my high school literary magazine, *Wings*—most under my name, though I did do a bit of "poetry ghost writing" for fellow classmates.

I still wrote in college, though not as much. I took a detour into drama, which deflected a lot of my creativity, earning a degree Theatre Arts with a dual major in acting and directing, and a minor in theatrical literature. I didn't go on in theater, but the training has definitely helped my writing.

After graduation, I got married, started a business with my husband, and gave birth to a child. When my son was around 10 years old, I began writing again. Stories and novels took up much of my writing time, though poems did still break through. Unfortunately, I lost the handwritten notebooks that held all my early poetry before I could transfer them to digital format. I'm hoping that someday I can discover old issues of *Wings* (my high school has closed, so there are no archives left) and recover at least some of these early works. They hold not only some good, and maybe even great, poems, but also a lot of wonderful memories.

My stories remained stashed in hand-written notebooks and in my computer until I divorced and moved to the West Coast. One day I saw a sign at my local library about SLO NightWriters, and decided to attend a meeting to see if it was something that might interest me.

I had just finished my first (publishable) novel, *Tangled Webs*, and wasn't sure what to do with it. Marilyn Meredith was the presenter at that meeting. She spoke about self-publishing and her experience with it. "I can do that," I thought. I went home, contacted Book Surge (eventually bought by Amazon and renamed Create Space), and the rest is history. This will be my fourteenth published book, and I have my own publishing company now.

Encouraged recently by a member of my critique group and a fantastic poet, Shirley Radcliff Bruton, I decided to put together the poems I still have into a little book, so I don't risk their being lost like my other ones. I've divided this volume into three sections:

1. General poems: Beginning with the first one I wrote, "Paradise," they run the gamut from haiku to epic-type poems, rhymed and free verse, with varying subject matters and themes. They're presented in no particular order.

2. For Ted: Poems dedicated to my brother, who committed suicide two days before my 25th birthday. His death devastated me, my family and all our friends. I still, and always will, miss him.

3. Song Lyrics: A somewhat new venture for me, begun when my mother requested I write a song for her funeral. I told her: a) if she died I'd never speak to her again, and b) I wrote poems, not songs. She said, "Oh, you can do it." The next week the entire song, words and melody to "I've Gone Home," flooded into my head. A few years later, I was able to sing it at her funeral, which I'm sure pleased her no end. I still don't know much about writing music, but these mostly spiritual songs just seemed to flow out of me. I do have music for each song, at least in my head, if not noted down on staff paper.

I hope you will enjoy these poems as much as I have enjoyed writing them.

An Eclectic Mix

Paradise

When you think of the word Paradise,
You may think of a quiet home,
Lying under a maple tree,
Or a holiday spent in Rome.

A fourth of July weekend,
Or fishing off a boat for cod,
But my idea of Paradise,
Is an evening spent with God.

Night Music

His fingers brush across
   the keyboard
      like sliding glissandos,
a twenty-first-century sonata
   in plastic,
the music of today
     cubicled
into isolated echoes;
staccato accents tapped with vigor
     against arrhythmic tempi
of printer
   phone line
      disk drive
         fluorescent lighting;
the muted cacophony
   of daily life.

I listen to his fingers,
   so square and strong,
a gentleness belied
by the sportsman's body,
listen to those fingers move
     amidst the figures and totals,

the reports and programs,
and I wonder how his fingers
   would move
in the darkness,
away from printer and
   phone line and disk drive,

Move in the private places of starlight,
   brush across
a human keyboard
   breathing syncopated rhythms
into the silence
   of life.

What would it sound like,
his music of the night?

Breaking Point

A little voice so like the tiny mustard seeds,
Planted deep in the insecurity it needs.
Festering and growing but never seeing light,
Surfacing only in the lonely dark of night.
Until the nearing future can no longer be ignored.
Until the nearing future strikes a warning chord.

A little voice so like the tiny mustard seeds,
A voice that has no words, but only fear;
A voice that rings its cry into the dark, the night,
Repeating to the world one single word:

—Help—

And no one does.

The following poem, "Centennial Dreams," was begun as part of an exercise at one of the SLO NightWriters monthly meetings. The then-current San Luis Obispo County Poet Laureate, Bonnie Young, showed us images of Arroyo Grande at the turn of the 20th century, and had us write down our impressions. The first stanza of this poem was written at that time.

I finished the poem at home, submitted it to the competition for the Centennial Celebration of Arroyo Grande, and won first place in my category! I was awarded a lovely medal, and "Centennial Dreams" joined the other winners in the time capsule, which is scheduled to be opened in 2111.

Centennial Dreams:

Looking back at 1911 from 2011

I wake with the dawn,
drapes opening to let in light
filtering between close-packed buildings
and closer-packed people
and smile at the centennial dress;

High-necked cotton organdy,
embroidered, ribbon-festooned,
worth a fortune these days,
flower-trimmed straw hat and high-button shoes
ready nearby for the celebration,
and think how quaint the town once was:
Space to breathe, to range, to live,
where life loomed large in its smallness,
bursting with promise and love.

I shed my daily synthetics,
and let yesterday's rare organics
kiss my body, warm my heart,
and smile in wonder that,
in the huge density of life today,
we clothe ourselves in the past to find
a way to reach out and grasp
the best of what the future has buried:
Space in which to become small again
and fulfill the promise of love.

For My Son, Aaron

I thought I knew,
        when it all began;
the story timeless, eternal.
All my hopes and prayers
        so clear,
a future set in love,
        like all the others.

And then
        a miracle intervened
and brought me you,
and my future opened
        into wondrous vistas
unimagined
in my wildest dreams.
A lifetime full of joy and awe,
        years of watching you
grow and become:
The child you were,
        The man you are,
The light you bring to the
        lives of others.

And I rise each day
	settled into
	the beauty of knowing
you are in the world.

Whine

My cat sighed out a whine
when I walked by her
and gazed at the softness
of her golden fur.

I wanted my fingers buried in it,
wanted her warm vibrating body
pressed to mine.

And she whined.

Was it a whine of desire
because she loves me, too?
Or because she's thinking,
"Not again;
Don't touch me!"

Whine.

The Miracle

The day was bright, the sun shone fair;
I saw a rainbow in my hair!
A single strand against the sky,
Myriad colors near my eye.
Numberless and flaming free,
a miracle, just for me.

Together

There the night, pale and waning
as though the dawn approached;
but never did it,

for you and I and the night
were one,
and darkness covered all,
forever.

Vertigo

The world spins around on its axis, they say,
But me, I've been spinning around the wrong way.
I stumble and stagger, like a sailor might do
When again on dry land after hoisting "a few".

Walls keep on moving, they get in my way;
I wish, like a dog, I could just tell them, "Stay!"
I bounce off of one, then the next and another;
Sometimes I wish I was just made of rubber.

My bruises have bruises cause the world won't
      stay put;
I can never be sure where I'm placing my foot.
Oh, my days are chock-full of struggle and strife,
But I just grin and bear it, cause this is my life.

The Garden Cat

You crouch and watch the world go past
safe on your miniature hillock
of purple ivy and white daisy,
eyes glowing amber,
surrounded by blooming geraniums
packed tight in an organic barrel of oak,
themselves captives of nature.

Clouds sail overhead,
headed for climes unknown and unknowable
—to you—
shedding slivers of the sky down
to kiss the earth with shadow.

An umbra dark as your luscious fur,
ebony light lifts the gentle breeze,
as it bows in obeisance
to the enthroned King
of a truncated empire,

bearing with it
the aroma of life—

the sound of birdcall,
the scurry of insect;
humanity encased in footsteps.

Life, in its enormity,
revolves around a corseting tether
that designates you,
The Garden Cat.

Book Covers

Busy world, busy lives…
Time
  Fleeting
    Pushing
      Rushing
Hurry! Hurry!
Glance at the covers
    Quick   hasty
Instant judgment

  -I am here-

Drawings, pictures
   Shapes...
Round
  Flat
    Substantial
      Ethereal

  -standing beside you-

entice and lure
    or

close the mind.
    Colors
swirling   brilliant
       soothing

  -can you see me?-

violent mixtures
      or
gentle blendings
    connect
with soul-deep
      emotion
   stir feelings
     or
   close the heart

  -look at me-

do you pause,
   slow down enough
to see   to read
to probe the depths…

I am here.
Do you see
   or do you judge?
Snap   snap

I am here
I am real
  I am not
    A
      Book
        Cover.

Dinner Time

set apart
we sit at tables,
   books propped upright,
open covers, turn pages
   as we eat,
immersing our lives
   into imaginary living

never looking up
meeting no one's eyes;
   connected in our isolation.
lonely women
cast aside by life.

we speak our dreams

into silence inhabited
   by paper people;
while through the diner windows
sun-washed warmth
   pours unfelt
upon our slashes of ink.
hearts beat on,
   laughter sounds;
not ours.

we sit sequestered
companioned by white pages,
   Like solitary spotlights;
cocooned within a writer's words,
a dreamer's life,
   searching for escape;
seeking connection
seeking purpose
without reaching for it;
   too afraid to take a breath
and let life have
another go at us.

I don't know why
   I ever learned to read.

Dreamscape

In the Divine
the night
she tells her tale

Captive,
I listen to her voice
patter like acid raindrops
against the window of my heart

grieving

oh, the children
who will never see
lives folded, alone
left where darkness rides the wind;
her words brittle leaves
crunched
beneath careless feet.

Hide
inside my arms;
take them
- take her -

be safe within the Light;
but the past rises,
reclaims its own;
dreams vanish unfulfilled

Darkness fades;
Divinity dies
Dawn breaks upon my
empty room,
and I mourn
the loss of the wind
on days when the rain doesn't fall

Luna Life

Open, moonflower,
Delicate pale miracle
Live the night for me.

Envy

She had a dream, she said,
after she read a poem
that left us all open-mouthed in awe,
a dream of words,
of bodies and walls,
of painting letters on rippling porous surfaces.
They became tattoos of hope, those words,
tattoos of love and joy,
and the words sank beneath flesh and brick
to entwine with the essence
of those bodies,
those walls.
They became one with a canvas of flesh and mortar,
their meanings now interwoven into
the lives of countless others
bringing them expansion and release.
A gift from her soul, to theirs.

But I, I do not dream of words.
I dream of bodies,
of sacrifice and fear and blood,
and alien dimensions rippling

as they intersect and interfere with life,
of hearts torn asunder as they search
for the meaning of who they are,
why they are.
And I gift my dreams in words
painted not on bodies and walls
but printed on paper and glass screens,
interactive dreams that
I hope will sink into minds, into hearts,
dreams that explore the limits of humanity,
and gift readers with ways of
being more than they were or could be,
by overcoming.

I envy her dreams, the words of hope
that she paints
across human canvasses.
I envy her talent
and the way her mind works.

Would anyone envy mine?

Everlasting

the telephone rings
    ~ anticipation ~
and my world falls apart

frozen in silence I listen
to the shape of days to come;
unwanted possibilities, endless in permutation

I've always known, without believing,
the time would come when life would change
    ~ ending ~
I've lived on days of borrowed light;
joy and laughter, safe in his love

now I sit, blinded, hand resting
on a phone that never should have rung
    ~ afraid ~
too far away to be there in anything but spirit
guilty that I am not at his bedside
terrified that he will leave before
    I can have one last kiss
        one final hug
        ~ alone ~

one last lucent touch
of his warm gentle hands on mine

there is a me that only he knows
a secret me that lives in the
soft silent spaces between us
      ~ hidden ~
a me that lives because he does;
a me that will be extinguished
when he is gone.

light fades as I relive a lifetime cradled
in his strength, his hope, his acceptance
      ~ everlasting ~
lasting only until the world changed
with just
    one
        phone call.

Becoming in Los Osos, CA

As I first drive up the hill, there on the left
fierce Oso rears upright;
carved bear of lumbering brown
huge forepaw raised—
in warning? or in welcome?
Guardian of the Valley
that hugs its secret places close
confounding even long-time residents
with dune-interrupted streets.

Wherever you want to go,
you can't get there from here

I never stopped to think
in my headlong rush across the country
craving adventure of the midlife crisis kind—
leaving behind all I loved and
denying the pain of it—
that people and towns are not the same
all over.
Unique, like snowflakes,
they defy newcomer expectations.

I thought I'd find what I left behind.

In the city, when I couldn't sleep,
there was always a sidewalk cafe open;
caffeine and traffic for company
during the faded-star nights.
But here they would roll up the sidewalks
—if they had any—
and send them to bed with the sun,
leaving the night to peaceful silence, long walks,
and firmament-embedded fireflies.

I knew three or four people once,
on the city street where I lived.
We even said hello a time or two.
The rest of us never exchanged a glance,
for there is danger in the looks of strangers.
You could love.
You could lose.
You live in fear.

But here in the place
where brown bears once roamed,
no one fears the loss.
Strangers greet each other like long-lost relatives,
become friends in supermarket lines,
expand their circles outward to embrace the valley world.

And beyond.

It terrified me at first, those smiles and waves,
strangers greeting me as though I belonged,
and was wanted.
Who are these people? I asked.
What do they want from me?
It spilled out of me, the anxiety of a city girl
self-transplanted from the madness
of big-city existence into small town life.

This was not what I left behind:
the family that had chosen me
so many years ago,
into which I never quite fit.
The fear of dark streets,
an obsession with shutters and locks.
An outsider always looking in.
Always loving, and losing.

This was more than I thought I would find:
a family of my own choosing,
an integration into a greater whole.
An embracing of the warm dark,
and trust once again come home to roost.
An insider embraced now with love.

This is life.

Today I hug deep inside me
the warm feeling of peace and belonging
that tells me I am where I need to be.
And in this small town, my town,
where I smile and wave back with joy
and pleasure—
for no one is a stranger here
in this Valley of the Bears—
I have finally discovered the meaning
of Life's grand design:

We sometimes let go of what we love
In order to simply love more.

Labyrinth Light

I remember, in years past…

   Walking the Labyrinth Path of
      Chartres laid out in the field by the pond:
   prickly dew-damp grass
      massaged my aching feet
   and slick mud squished
      between my squeamish toes
   as my pedal digits finger-painted across the ground
        and winged blessings showered down
          from feathered throats above.
   I heard sun-kissed morning greetings
      soft laughter, murmurs in the distance
   a coiled counterpoint to the winding flow
      of feeling, thought and breath
   as the sanctity of the Path wafted
its circular way
      deep into the core of my clouded soul.

      Revelation without Light.

It's gone now, the Labyrinth moved inside,

    embraced within the darkness of walls,
        submerged into a future that
birthed this day. I hear:
    The soft susurration of bare feet
tracing the indoor path,
    sans sunlight, mud and grass
my unshod soles slide over hotel carpeting
    along a Labyrinth of love
an artificial path that has somehow wound me
    beyond the darkness of my life,
        past blind revelation;
   and here
beneath a gaudy chandelier
    revealing light births this day of wonderment
        at who I am,
            who I am become.

Within the walls, within the darkness:

    Labyrinth Light.

Love Story

I want to live inside you.

> I want to know who gets the piece
>   of you
> you keep so far from me.

I want to take Eden from my pocket
> and spread it at your feet.

Look close;
> what we get
>   is never what we see
> and what we see is
>   rarely what we get.

Magic is,
> it makes the living real.
> The rituals that bind us
>   set us free.

I will never let you go.

Mirror Eyes

deep beneath mirror eyes
a woman lies
imprisoned.
alone, unknown.
pinioned
beneath the weight
of years

buried beneath
an avalanche
of expectation unmet.

forlorn.

abandoned
by life,
like the scruffled dresses
of childhood;

discarded,
like hair ribbons
frayed and worn…

there was laughter once,
and promise.
there was future,
dreams of hope
of love
of life

now in those eyes,
those mirror eyes,
deep within
the hard glass,
not even the echoes
of promise remain,
no light, no love,
the way so long lost
it might never have begun
at all.

To whom do you
reach out,
where do you
turn,
when no one is there?

To whom can you cry?
Mirror eyes

Mourning

He shakes his head;
   he could not sleep – again.

In silence he molds the dark,
planning ways to hurt me.
   He must,
   for he does it so easily, so often.

It does not take much these days.

He turns away, and
pain widens, breath by breath,
like ripples in a pool of blood.
       Whose?

In my own private dark
I examine the why's of my life
   and find I can no longer see;
   can no longer be.

I do not even think
   that I love him anymore.

One Fond Farewell

Long are the chains that bind a heart
To something here and now;
Little things so truly meant
Are swiftly gone, somehow.

You've grown, O Tree, who walks away,
You've blossomed silent sound;
And now your words have scattered wide
Love's message on the ground.

These little seeds you've nourished so,
Great bushes we will be;
It takes a truly human heart
To change humanity.

To leave behind a tear, a sigh,
The task of common men;
But here you've left a piece of you
Until you come again.

One Spring

The rains failed
one Spring
and the land perished.

We walked to the river bank;
devastation
and death
wherever we looked.

Then
he took my hand
and went down
on one knee
in the dry river bed

lined with
   cracked rocks
      dead algae
         dried fish bones,

and asked me to reach
for life.

With him.

Soft Skin

I remember
my mother's skin
as she aged,
so delicate and soft,
like stroking clouds
or the down
on a new-born baby's head;
a touch of Heaven as she
neared her entrance into that
august Palace,
a reminder that soon she
would be far beyond my touch.
Far beyond my presence.

Now as I stroke the underside
of my own arm
and feel that same softness,
that same delicacy,
I wonder how
I got to this place
of endings,

my own body slipping
down the road of no return,
never enquiring if my spirit
wants to accompany it.

Greedy in its desire
to follow its own path,
my body bows to years that
my conscious mind discounts—
uncaring of the years yet to come,
the things still to accomplish—
pulling me where
I do not want to go,
where I cannot imagine
myself venturing,
not for decades to come.

If ever.

How strange
and somehow fitting
that both the beginning
and the ending
encapsulate themselves
in delicate softness,
when death—
unlike the space in between—

is so harsh,
so heart-stoppingly feared,
so final.

Do we simply come from
the softness of nothing
to slip into
the wonder and bustle of life,
then vanish back into the
nothing of softness?

I do not want
to be beyond the touch,
beyond the present.

And still my skin softens.
It softens.

Storm Surge

It started in October,
as though I had turned one of life's
invisible corners,
and one-by-one
along this new street
I ran headlong into
circumstances
that had crouched in wait
for just the right time.

Destruction in perfect order:
This because of this because of this,
dominoes of the physical kind,
until my life
was turned upside down.

I look at people around me
and see
that this is nothing new.
It's just age taking control,
the downslope of a hill
I didn't know I'd climbed,

a hill
I refused to see
until I had no choice.

But there's no help for it.
The future,
with all it entails,
rises up
and rolls over us
with the tenacity of a tidal wave,
leaving behind
in the debris
opportunities to be
and to become more.

But differently.

When the Perfect Storm of Age
rages unchecked
the best that
human shipmates can do
is cling to life's masthead
with both hands and feet
and enjoy the rollicking ride.

Summer Place

Dilapidated, shingled roof of green;
A musty yard begs little feet to roam.
The long-abandoned place stands sad, serene;
So dank and cold, and yet so like a home.

A faded rose, a tarnished silver knife;
Papers, books, the treasures of her store,
Packed up with love and care they taste of life;
The life of Anna, who comes back no more.

By the fire I read the words she'd said;
I seem to feel her presence quite nearby.
Nonsense! They're just remnants of the dead;
Yet with each toss I hear her anguished cry.

And I think while watching flames eat hungrily,
That someday someone will burn my memory.

Premonition

I sit and watch my family dear,
Or hear the words that I should hear,
And yet I feel so all alone:
In my heart seeds of truth are sown.

I feel apart from friend and foe,
I fear I have no place to go.
I fear my life with dust soon blends:
I fear my fear, it never ends.

It sears my heart, this vision's game,
I know it's true, and death's its name.
And deep within my heart I cry,
Oh no, it's not my time to die.

There's something that I have to do,
It's something good and something true.
But as I take another breath,
I know that I am near my death.

Musing On The Muse

Jet plane
   in the place of nowhere,
Idling on tarmac silver-bright
   in moonlit darkness;
Wingéd thoughts
      Hovering
   Just beyond my reach,
      Reaching
Deep within my heart.
      Bypassing
Mind
   Words
      Thought
         Logic
A mind-meld I cannot feel
In words I cannot hear

      I am here
        I am here

Will we fly upon
   Your silver wings,

Journeys everlasting
    Through an instant of time?
Will you take me
   To the place of somewhere
     The place my soul resides?
Can we cross the barrier of
     Separate dreams
And stitch together into Oneness
   The planes of lives untold?

Can we unfold?
   I am here
     I am here.

Boredom

Boredom
    is a bore.

It leaves you
   bored
     and
Boredom leads...

    to...
        more...
            Boredom
    until
you are immersed
        in the
Doms
    of
        Bore…

So boringly bored
        that
even your
        Boredom
            is
            bored:
bored-bored-bored, bored-bored

Oh, Boredom is boring
        so very, very boring

boring, boring, boring…

Almost as boring
        as this
dumb, boring poem.
        Ho-hum…

Perambulations

Dost thou thinketh me canst writeth?
So dost otherths, yea, forsooth.
Me canst writeth all long dayeth
Stuffeth that ist quel tres cooth.

Me ben rhymin' words with timin',
Me ben playin' wit me youth.
There ain't nutten me can't button
Up wit pen and tongue in tooth.

If thou thinketh ye can readeth
And a glimmer glimpse of truth,
Ye are deadeth in the headeth –
Ain't no meanin' in this booth!

For Ted

Consequences

I remember a butterball
Who snuggled in my bed,
When the winter nights were cold;
A nightcap on his head.

As we grew up he'd whisper low,
His lips upon my ear,
The special secrets dear to him
And that I longed to hear.

But something changed for him and me;
It's not the same, today.
My caustic words and flighty moods
Drove him far away.

He watches me through shielded eyes
And keeps his heart locked tight.
He doesn't speak until I ask
And then his words are slight.

Is there no hope for us at all?
Is this how life shall go?
Shall I never win back to me
The brother I used to know?

The Corridor of Time

I stand on the far side
of the corridor of time
     looking back
wondering how changed
     the shape
of life's spiraling dance
would be
     had you lived.

Swirling through what ifs
I trip on hours of guilt,
days of regret
reaping reward through
     random movement,

never knowing if I am enough;
   could have been,
      would have been...

The trail of never wills
widen
as each year sarabands
into lives unlived,
   and my life unfolds
      alone,
here on the far side
of the corridor of time.

Aftermath

I woke up one morning not long ago
to find that forgiveness
   like a thief in the night
had stolen unaware into my life,
   and with gentle stealth
drained off the anger,
   evaporated the misery,

        eased away the pain—
bit by bit
    ounce by ounce
        drop by drop.

Here now, on the far side
of suicide's aftermath,
    with that fateful night still so clear
in my memory
    in my heart
        in my dreams
I discover that I forgave you
    —unbeknownst to me—
        years ago.

Yet still the pain lingers,
    pulsing in time to my heartbeat:
        Life's rhythm of sorrow and guilt.

What could I have done?
What should I have done?

It seems it is myself
    I cannot forgive.

The Night of Blood

The blood I didn't see
—couldn't see—
shone in the darkness
on the night we sat
in the
—brilliance—
      of the waiting room,
until the doctor came in,
scrubs still pristine blue,
—bloodless—
      and told us he was gone.

And my heart bled.

For Ted

Each endless year

Summer fades
   to pale ashes;
Heat-baked clay
and torpid nights
   of wonder.

I wonder...

   Memories of you
twine through my mind
parched, arid dreams that die
   between
shadows' cold remains.

Reaching out
I touch the breast of life
   to find
chalk-dust death upon my fingers.

Good-bye is too hard a word to say.

Come back...

Summer of '72

I watched you
through days of unspoken anguish,
    months of silent pain
  unasked questions
crowding your teasing eyes.

And I did not see.

I made you into who I
wanted you to be,
quiet little brother grown,
    so proud of the man
  you'd become,
And watched with giddy glee
  the girls
    drawn
to your lighted soul
    all that summer long.

Or was it the aura of
Little-Boy-Lost,
  so subtle I was unaware,
or a darkness hidden deep

beneath layers of devil-may-care,
that moth-fluttered souls
     younger than I
   —more perceptive than I—
to the fragile flame
of you…

I did not see
though I looked and smiled
   and laughed
      and dreamed…

So unaware.

Where were you that summer,
while your body surfed the waves
    and drank the sun
  and turned so many heads,
and your smile gladdened hearts
    and quickened dreams,
  and your humor lured
the beach-world to your feet?

Where were you
that you could not speak,
  could not reach out,
could not trust or share.
    Could not live.

And now I see, eyes open at last,
heart yearning
    hungering for a future
        foreshortened...

I see now, my eyes wide open
    with nothing left to see...
        too late.

And still I wonder:
Where were you?
    Where are you now?

Edward Latchford Tuttle, Jr.
October 16, 1950 — August 18, 1972

Song Lyrics

The Dream of Love

Looking for my heart, dreaming of a life
Searching for my soul, being who I am
All that I will find...
Because I walked away.

On the road to somewhere
Alone I lost my way
On that road I found you
And thought that I could stay

I held you in my heart
Among the clouds of night
But dreams are made for darker times
And I must live in light

For life was made for giving
To hope and laugh and share
Or it's not worth the living
And all that's left is air

If we're not right
Then it's not right
The dream was love
That never was,
So I must walk away.

All You Can Give Me

Stand out of my pathway, my darling,
Get out of my one exit door.
I have to be moving along now,
I'll never be back anymore.

I'm chasing a feeling elusive,
That settles on rainbows above,
I need something you cannot offer;
All you can give me is love.

It may lie around nearby corners,
It may lie a country away.
It won't let me rest 'til I find it;
It dictates my will and my way.

I need all those wide-flowing rivers,
I need silver rainbows above.
I need something you cannot offer;
All you can give me is love.

> I thought you would be
> The man of my dreams,
> But I can't live on love alone,
> At least that's how it seems.

Don't block up the doorway, my darling,
I can't take you with me this time.
The road isn't one for the sharing.
The mountain is just mine to climb.

My heart is so heavy with yearning,
A whip in a velvet glove.
I need something you cannot offer;
All you can give me is love.

I need something you cannot offer;
All you can give me is love.

Be Still

      Be still, and know that I am God
      Be still, and know that I Am

I dwell in the silence,
In the space between
The moments of your day.
There you will find me in the stillness
Waiting for you.

      Be still, and know that I am God
      Be still, and know that I Am

Listen to the silence.
Let the world around
You stop and fade away.
Then you will hear my voice in stillness,
Calling your name.

      Be still, and know that I am God
      Be still, and know that I Am

I come with the sunrise,
In the pause between
The darkness and the light.
There you will sense the words I give you,
To guide your way.

>   Be still, and know that I am God
>   Be still, and know that I Am

When darkness has fallen,
I will come and sit
In stillness at your side.
There you will know me in the quiet,
And share my love.

>   Be still, and know that I am God
>   Be still, and know that I Am

He Knows

Secrets, deep within in my heart I hold secrets
That I never want, anyone to know,
They shame me so.

Moments, how they haunt me all of those
      moments,
When I turned my head, didn't want to see.
Oh, was that me? But…

> He knows, my God knows,
> And He loves me anyway,
> Loves me more than words can say,
> For He died to set me free,
> Yes, He loves me.

Forgive them, I just cannot seem to forgive them,
For the hurt they've caused, the pain deep in my
      heart
Tears me apart.

Anger, how I hold onto all my anger,
Let my temper rule, such ugly things I have said
I hang my head. Still…

> He knows, my God knows,
> And He loves me anyway,
> Loves me more than words can say,
> For He died to set me free,
> Yes, He loves me.

Silent, if I don't tell and I stay silent,
My friends will never know, how I've failed to be,
What I should be.

Trembling, in my heart I feel only trembling.
How could anyone love this secret me,
If they did see. Yet…

> He knows, my God knows,
> And He loves me anyway,
> Loves me more than words can say,
> For He died to set me free,
> Yes, He loves me.

Journey, oh so sweet and strange, life's a journey,
Everyday a new lesson to be learned.
But do I learn?

Walking, along God's path I will keep walking
And though I stumble through the seeds that have
    been sown,
I'm not alone. For…

He knows, my God knows,
And He loves me anyway,
Loves me more than words can say,
For He died to set me free,
Yes, He loves me.

Take My Hand, O Lord

> Take my hand, O Lord, and walk with me
> Teach me your way.
> Take my hand, O Lord, and lead me
> In the peace of your love day by day.

Long are the nights of my sorrow,
Sweet are the prayers that I pray,
Strong is my hope in tomorrow,
For you stand beside me all the way.

> Take my hand, O Lord, and walk with me
> Teach me your way.
> Take my hand, O Lord, and lead me
> In the peace of your love day by day.

Guide me as we walk together,
Through this world of toil and strife,
I know I will never be abandoned,
For you are my way and my life.

> Take my hand, O Lord, and walk with me
> Teach me your way.
> Take my hand, O Lord, and lead me
> In the peace of your love day by day.

Wrap your loving arms around me,
Bless me with your presence true,
For you are my comfort and my savior,
I lift up my heart in praise to you.

> Take my hand, O Lord, and walk with me
> Teach me your way.
> Take my hand, O Lord, and lead me
> In the peace of your love day by day.

Come to the Table of Love

> Drink this wine and eat this food,
> Come to the Table of Love
> Taste and see that the Lord is good,
> Come to the Table of Love

God has given us treasure,
More precious than silver and gold
He gave His Son so that we could live;
Love made the story unfold.

> Drink this wine and eat this food,
> Come to the Table of Love
> Taste and see that the Lord is good,
> Come to the Table of Love

Grains and milk and honey,
Will keep the body whole,
But the meal we share at this table today,
Will nourish both spirit and soul.

> Drink this wine and eat this food,
> Come to the Table of Love
> Taste and see that the Lord is good,
> Come to the Table of Love

We do not walk in darkness,
Nor live by bread alone,
The word of God sustains our life,
For He has made us His own.

> Drink this wine and eat this food,
> Come to the Table of Love
> Taste and see that the Lord is good,
> Come to the Table of Love

Feed the hungry beggar,
Take care of the sick and the poor,
The love that we give to all humankind,
Will open God's heavenly door.

> Drink this wine and eat this food,
> Come to the Table of Love
> Taste and see that the Lord is good,
> Come to the Table of Love

Come my brothers and sisters,
Partake in the feast of the King,
He shed His blood on the cross for us,
Of Christ and His Glory we sing!

> Drink this wine and eat this food,
> Come to the Table of Love
> Taste and see that the Lord is good,
> Come to the Table of Love

Love One Another

> Love one another as I have loved you,
> Love one another as I have loved you.

I walked among you, then on the cross I died,
Still I walk among you, in spirit at your side,
Can you understand the depth of Love I have for you,
If you would remember me, this is what you do,

> Love one another as I have loved you,
> Love one another as I have loved you.

Picture in your mind how bright the spirit glows,
When you light the spark of grace, from which
    true beauty flows,
The secret lies within you, deep within your heart,
Joy can be your daily fare, this is how you start,

> Love one another as I have loved you,
> Love one another as I have loved you.

Can you imagine, a world that has no war,
Can you imagine, no lock on any door,
No pain, no fear, no poverty, yes, you can make it true,
If you want to change the world, this is what you do,

> Love one another as I have loved you,
> Love one another as I have loved you.

Show the world true Spirit by your actions everyday,
Example teaches more than all our words could ever say,
We are the emissaries God has put upon this earth,
The teachings of Lord Jesus Christ, will give Shalom full birth.

> Love one another as I have loved you,
> Love one another as I have loved you.

Come Worship Our God

Day Version:

Awake from your slumber, morning has broken,
God has brought the light.
Let all creation now with one voice
Worship and praise His name.

A rise from your bed, come into the light,
God's love is waiting here.
Join in the chorus of angel song and
Worship our God most high.

> Everything that God has made,
> throughout the Universe,
> Is but a faint reflection of
> the Glory of His Love.

Come to the Lord, the giver of life,
With humble heart and mind,
Gather together here in His house
To worship and praise the Lord.
Come worship and praise His Name.

Night Version:

Rest from your labors, slumber is near,
God has brought the night
Let all creation now with one voice,
Worship and praise His name.

Come welcome the stars with wonder and awe
God's love is waiting here
Join now together, lift up your voice,
To worship our God most high.

> Everything that God has made,
> throughout the universe
> Is but a faint reflection of
> the Glory of His Love

Slumber in peace wrapped safe in His arms
And trust that the day will come.
Stand with your family, gathered here now,
To worship and praise the Lord
Come worship and praise His name.

I Am the Way

I am the Way, I am the Truth,
I am the Way, I am the Life,
If you take my hand and walk with me,
we can teach the world to love.

I am the Way, I am your hope,
I am the Truth, I am your faith,
If you take my hand and walk with me,
we can build a world of love.

> I am the way, I am the truth, I am the life
> Those who believe in Me shall never die

I am the Way, I am the sun,
I am the Life, I am the rain,
If you take my hand and walk with me,
we will fill the world with love.

I am the Way, I am the morn,
I am the Truth, I am the night,
If you take my hand and walk with me,
we can sow the world with love.

I am the Way, I am your tears,
I am the Life, I am your joy,
If you take my hand and walk with me,
we can lead the world to love.

> I am the way, I am the truth, I am the life
> Those who believe in Me shall never die

I am the Way, I am the dark,
I am the Truth, I am the light,
If you take my hand and walk with me,
we will reap a world of love.

I am the Way, I am the moon,
I am the Life, I am the stars.
If you take my hand and walk with me,
we can hold the world in love.

I am the Way, I am the might,
I am the Truth, I am the power,
If you take my hand and walk with me,
we can change the world with love.

> Take my hand, walk with me,
> follow my word, and you will live forever.

You Are A Lamp

You are a lamp, unto my feet
You guide my steps, You light my path
I need not fear the darkness now
You are a lamp, unto my feet.

When all my dreams have turned to dust,
When all my hope has gone away
You take my hand and lead me on
You guide me safe to journey's end.

And when I wander in the dark
Your Word shines forth into my heart
Your living water gives me life
You are a lamp unto my feet.

Too often, Lord, I lose my way
In dark despair I feel alone,
But when I look you're always there,
A light to lead me home to you.

You are a lamp unto my feet
A hand to hold, a love to trust
A beacon that is always there
You are a lamp, unto my feet
You are a lamp, unto my feet.

Where Will He Be Born Tonight?

Jesus Christ, our risen savior,
Born a babe in Bethlehem,
Prince of Peace, our Father's favor,
Heralded through an angel's hymn
>Tiny infant in a manger
>Born to set my spirit free
>My life, my friend,
>my strength in peril,
>Living now, inside of me.

King of Kings, almighty God,
Counselor and Star of Morn,
You opened wide our Father's heart,
On the night that you were born.
>Tiny infant in a manger
>Born to set my spirit free
>My life, my friend,
>my sanctuary,
>Living now, inside of me.

Guiding wise men, star of wonder,
Onward through a world of strife,
Shining on God's gift to mankind,
Soon to be the Way of Life.

> Tiny infant in a manger
> Born to set my spirit free
> My life, my friend,
> my inspiration,
> Living now, inside of me.

Not one had room, a lowly stable,
Was the first thing in God's sight,
Are we any different now,
Where will He be born tonight?
> Tiny infant in a manger
> Born to set my spirit free
> My life, my friend,
> my destination,
> Living now, inside of me.

Jesus Christ, an infant born,
In a stable dark and forlorn,
Waits for us with Love pure and bright;
Where will He be born tonight?

<u>(Christmas Day Ending)</u>

Not one had room, a lowly stable
Was the place God had to stay,
Are we any different now,
Where will He be born today?

> Tiny infant in a manger
> Born to set my spirit free
> My life, my friend,
> my destination,
> Living now, inside of me.

Jesus Christ, an infant born
In a stable dark and forlorn
Waits for us to show us the way,
Where will He be born today?

(Christmas Season Ending)

Not one had room, a lowly stable
Was the place God had to stay;
Are we any different now,
Is there room in you today?
> Tiny infant in a manger
> Born to set my spirit free
> My life, my friend,
> my destination,
> Living now, inside of me.

Jesus Christ, an infant born
In a stable dark and forlorn
Waits for us with Love pure and true;
Will you let Him live in you?

Christmas Is For Children

When I was a youngster,
Christmas was a treat,
Full of fun and laughter,
And reindeer's tiny feet,
I had no thought of Jesus,
Born to set me free,
I only saw the magic,
And presents 'neath the tree.

And then as I grew older,
It lost its magic spell,
Christmas is for children,
The world knows that so well,
By emptiness surrounded,
I passed each Christmas day,
Longing for the childhood,
I'd left along the way.

But somehow Jesus found me,
He took the pain away,
He filled my heart with laughter,
And childhood's gentle play,
I've been reborn God's child,
I know who Jesus is,
My God, my Life, my Savior,
Here in me He lives.

And Christmas is for children,
Hear the angel's song,
Wide-eyed awesome wonder,
Lasting all year long,
Voices sweetly ringing,
All in one accord,
Yes, Christmas is for children,
The children of the Lord.

Christmas is for children,
The children of the Lord.

I've Gone Home

(written for my mother, Shirley Young Tuttle)

I am a child of hope and peace,
Part of the Master Plan
I was sent to earth to learn to love,
And to share my heart and hand,
Now I've gone home, I've gone home,
Let the trumpet sound, call the victory,
For God was waiting there for me.

Made in His image, body and soul,
I lived and learned and grew,
Though I failed at times to follow His way,
Somehow I always knew,
That I'd go home, I'd go home,
Where my Father stands, radiantly,
Waiting patiently for me.

God tested me throughout my life,
Some lessons hard to bear,
Still I walked the road in trust and faith,
For I knew my God was there,
Saying you'll come home, someday you'll come home,
There'll be joy and praise and angel song,
for you'll be back where you belong.

God graced my soul with love and joy,
And He danced on the night I was born.
Then He sent His angels to watch over me;
There is nothing here to mourn,
For I've gone home, I've gone home,
Let the trumpet sound, call the victory,
For God was waiting there for me.

Though it's hard, I know, for you who stay,
Upon this world of strife,
Take comfort in the love we shared,
And celebrate my life.
You know that I've gone home, I've gone home,
And when the day has come that your journey's
 through,
I will be waiting there for you.

Yes, I've gone home, I've gone home
And with my God I stand, hand in hand,
Waiting patiently for you.

About the Author

Susan Tuttle grew up in Buffalo, New York, and has lived in New England; Lexington, KY; and Ossining, NY. In 2004 she picked up and drove across the country, landing on the Central Coast of California where she lives in a small town whose motto is: Wherever you want to go, you can't get there from here. (Yes, she coined it after getting detoured by numerous sand dunes.) She has found her passion and her place there, in the valley where the weather is always perfect—even when it isn't.

After landing on the California coast, she discovered and got involved in San Luis Obispo (SLO) NightWriters, the premier writing organization on the Central Coast that is home to a varied, welcoming and warm group of writers (www.slonightwriters.org). She has served as president, secretary and treasurer, and currently is newsletter editor and offers critiques before the monthly meetings.

Susan is also a member of Sisters in Crime (SinC) National, the Central Coast Chapter of SinC (she currently serves as treasurer and newsletter editor), and the Public Service Writers Association (PSWA). She is also the owner of WriterWithin Publications, an independent publishing company. (www.WriterWithinPubs.com).

A professional editor and writing teacher, Susan is an award-winning author who writes in various genres: suspense, mystery, fantasy, sci-fi and young adult, as well as nonfiction articles. She has produced a 6-volume workbook series for writers of fiction and creative nonfiction titled *Write It Right,* based on the weekly classes she teaches.

Under the pen name Susan Grace O'Neill, she has published the first of six volumes of spiritual meditations on the Parables, and a book on journeying with Jesus through Lent.

Her fiction and nonfiction work has garnered numerous awards and has appeared in Mind Prints Literary Journal, Tolosa Press, Simply Clear Media & Marketing (formerly Tolosa Press), If & When Literary Journal, The Feathered Flounder Literary Journal, and Central Coast Kind Magazine.

Susan is currently working on a new series set in the town she lives in, featuring Skylark, a private investigator who has psychic abilities, two young adult fantasy series, and other stand-alone stories. She lives with her imaginary cat in a house filled with her (mostly unfinished) handmade quilts and (mostly finished) knitted scarves. You can find her on Facebook (susanwriter), Twitter (stuttlewriter), Goodreads, LinkedIn, and her website/blog, www.SusanTuttleWrites.com. She loves hearing from her readers.

Publications

Fiction (writing as Susan Tuttle):
    Suspense: *Tangled Webs*
                       Piece By Piece
                       Sins of the Past
    Paranormal Suspense:
                       Proof of Identity
    Historical Suspense:
                       A Matter of Identity
    Short Mystery Stories:
                       Death in the Valley

(All available in print from Amazon and as Kindle e-books. *Proof of Identity* and *Sins of the Past* also available as audio books)

Poetry (available in print from Amazon):
    Mirror Eyes

The Tiny Tales 5-Minute or Less Reads for Busy People Series (in print from Amazon):
    Tiny Tales: Flash Fiction
    Tiny Tales: Mystery/Suspense
    Tiny Tales: Sci-fi/Fantasy
    Tiny Tales: Skylark, PI
    Tiny Tales: Romancing the Muse

Susan's short works appear in the following Anthologies:
>*Somewhere in Crime*
>*The Best of SLO NightWriters in Tolosa Press*
>*Deadlines: Murder and Mayhem on the California Coast, Vol. 1*
>*Deadlines: Murder and Mayhem on the California Coast, Vol. 2*
>*Tales from a Rocky Coast, Vol. 1*

Non-Fiction (available in print from Amazon):
***Write It Right Workbook* Series:**
>*Workbook #1: Character, Setting, Story*
>*Workbook #2: Point of View (POV)*
>*Workbook #3: Plot, Dialogue*
>*Workbook #4: Scenes, Style/Voice*
>*Workbook #5: Conflict/Tension, Subplot*
>*Workbook #6: Brilliant Beginnings, Extraordinary Endings*

Writing as Susan Grace O'Neill:
Spiritual Meditations: The Journey Series
>*Lord, Let Me Grow: A Journey with Jesus through the Parables, Vol. 1*

Susan Tuttle

Lord, Let Me Walk: A 3-Year Journey with Jesus through Lent

(Available in print from Amazon)

Works in Progress:
    The Skylark PI Series:
        Vol. 1: *Tough Blood*
        Vol. 2: *Words Left Unsaid*
        Vol. 3: *Death Duties*
        Vol. 4: *The SomeWhen Murder*
        Vol. 5: *Dead Ringer*
    Skylark Companion Books:
        The Eyes of Death (Mackienzie Straite)
        Not Even Death (Linnea Keszeli)
        The Unhonored Past (Lillia)

    YA/Adult Books in Progress:
        Destany's Daughter Series
            Vol. 1: *The One*
            Vol. 2: *The Restoral*
        Demon's Run Series
            Vol. 1: *A Deadly Shade of Gray*

    Adult Fantasy:
        Stealing Shyon
        The CPW Series:
            Vol. 1: *Cursed in California*

www.ingramcontent.com/pod-product-compliance
Lightning Source LLC
Chambersburg PA
CBHW030002050426
42451CB00006B/90